# HEADSTART HISTORY PAPERS

## William Cecil, Lord Burghley: Minister of Elizabeth I

by

## A.G.R. Smith

# HEADSTART HISTORY

Published by     HEADSTART HISTORY
                 PO Box 41, Bangor, Gwynedd, LL57 1SB

Set by           C.B.S.
                 155 Hamilton Road,
                 Felixstowe, Suffolk, IP11 7DR

Printed by       THE IPSWICH BOOK COMPANY LTD
                 The Drift, Nacton Road,
                 Ipswich, Suffolk IP3 3QR


ISBN             1 873041 20 9

A CIP catalogue record for this book is available from the British Library.

# CONTENTS

Frontispiece :     William Cecil, Lord Burghley
on his mule.
By courtesy of The Marquess
of Salisbury

# INTRODUCTION

The HEADSTART HISTORY PAPERS aim to identify themes and topics the significance of which extends beyond the studies of professional historians. The papers are distillations of the research of distinguished scholars in a form appropriate to students and to the general reader.

William Cecil, Lord Burghley has an unchallenged reputation as one of the greatest statesmen of the sixteenth century. Thomas Cromwell had guided Henry VIII in bringing about the break with Rome, and had subjected the Church of England to the Crown and in doing so had created an English 'nation-state' subject to no foreign power.

Cecil's ability had been recognised by Northumberland under Edward VI and in 1558 his undoubted integrity had been recognised by Elizabeth. Whatever their differences of opinion, the Queen and her minister were in fundamental agreement. When she appointed him to her Council and made him Secretary of State she never had cause to alter her initial appraisal:-

> 'This judgment I have of you that you will not be corrupted by any manner of gift and that you will be faithful to the state...''

Despite his early reservations about Elizabeth, in later life his own judgement of the Queen was there was never so wise a woman born. Queen and Minister were in fundamental agreement and their unique and lasting relationship was to dominate the second half of the sixteenth century. Dr. Smith points out that 'the contributions which they made to the Elizabethan Age were so often made together that it is very difficult to give either one of them priority of achievement over the other.'

Alan Smith has been in the Department of History at the University of Glasgow for thirty years, and is currently Reader. His early research was supervised in London by Joel Hursfield but then he returned to Glasgow where he had pursued his undergraduate studies.

Dr. Smith has published widely on the Tudor period and two of those works have been of outstanding value to students - *The Government of Elizabethan England* and *The Emergence of a Nation State*. He has recently published *Tudor Government* for the Historical Association and now joins other established scholars in the distinguished list of HEADSTART HISTORY PAPERS. It is a pleasure to thank Dr. Smith for his contribution to the series.

Judith Loades.
Bangor, 1991

# AUTHOR'S NOTE

In this pamphlet William Cecil, who was created Lord Burghley in 1571, is sometimes referred to as Cecil, sometimes as Burghley. His younger son and political heir is always referred to as Robert Cecil.

In November 1558, soon after her succession to the throne, Queen Elizabeth indicated that William Cecil was to be her chief adviser. It was the beginning of a remarkable partnership which was to last - virtually uninterrupted - for almost forty years, right up to the time of Cecil's death in August 1598. It is this period of service, unparalleled either before or since in English history, which has brought Cecil, who became Lord Burghley in 1571, enduring historical fame. His career after Elizabeth's accession can, however, only be fully understood after an analysis of some of the major influences on his life before 1558.

## I. APPRENTICESHIP

Cecil was born at Bourne in Lincolnshire in September 1520 into a middling gentry family.[1] He was initially educated at nearby grammar schools at Grantham and Stamford and in May 1535, when he was still only fourteen - not an exceptional age for university students at the time - was admitted to St John's College, Cambridge. His studies at Cambridge brought him into contact with scholars like John Cheke and Roger Ascham, both of them St John's men, and in Cheke he found not only a tutor but also an intimate friend and future brother-in-law who was the greatest Greek scholar of the day in England. One of Cecil's biographers - almost certainly his secretary Michael Hickes - who wrote an account of

---

1 Details of Burghley's private and public life can be found in C. Read, *Mr Secretary Cecil and Queen Elizabeth* (1955), *Lord Burghley and Queen Elizabeth* (1960) - hereafter Read, i, ii - and in B.W. Beckingsale, *Burghley, Tudor Statesman* (1967).

2

his character and career soon after his death, remarked on his astonishing powers of work, even at that early stage in his life. When he was at St John's he hired the bellringer 'to call him up at four of the clock every morning, with which watching and continual sitting there fell abundance of humours into his legs, then very hardly cured.'[2] These humours may have been the origins of the gout which plagued him in his later years, but at the time they bore witness to his love for scholarship and the scholarly life, a love which remained with him throughout his career. Ascham's remark that 'in the fairest spring that ever there was of learning' he was 'one of the forwardest young plants in all that worthy college of St John's' was made after Cecil had become Elizabeth's principal minister and chancellor of Cambridge university, but it tells us something about his reputation and helps to explain his patronage of scholars, like the historian William Camden, in his later years. The Cambridge of the 1530s was a place of Protestant influence as well as humanistic learning and Cecil seems to have been confirmed there in the moderate but committed Protestantism which he was to maintain throughout his life.

His entry to Gray's inn in 1541 gave him an opportunity to acquire some knowledge of the English common law. Most gentlemen in that litigious age became involved in lawsuits at some time in their careers and it became more and more common as the century progressed for members of the gentry to spend some time at one of the

2 A.G.R. Smith, *The 'Anonymous Life' of William Cecil, Lord Burghley* (Lampeter, 1990), 43 - 4. For the identification of Hickes as the almost certain author, 9ff. It will be assumed from now on in the text that Hickes was the author.

four inns of Court, where they could imbibe at least some knowledge of legal procedures. Life in London, of course, exposed them to the temptations of the metropolis and we know that Cecil, who had a reputation for 'witty mirth and merry temper' in his younger days, succumbed to at least one of them. He gambled heavily and lost all his money, bedding and books to a friend, though eventually he recovered his property through an ingenious piece of trickery.[3] He took a gamble of another kind three months later. In August 1541, when he was still only twenty, he married Mary Cheke, the sister of his friend and mentor John Cheke. The lady brought with her only a small dowry and the marriage seems to have been a love match, one of the few rash actions of Cecil's long life. She gave birth to a son, Thomas, in 1542 and died during the following year. His remarriage in 1545 was a much more sober affair. The bride was Mildred Cooke, one of the four learned daughters of Sir Anthony Cooke, governor to the young Prince Edward. She bore him a son, Robert, and two daughters, Anne and Elizabeth, and ran his household with admirable efficiency and good sense until her death in 1589.

The death of Henry VIII in 1547 provided the opportunity for Cecil to achieve political prominence. The virtual *coup d'état* at the end of Henry's reign which ensured the victory of the Protestant party headed by Edward Seymour, earl of Hertford and uncle to the young king, and Archbishop Cranmer made it clear that there would soon be substantial changes in the religious life of the country. In these circumstances it is not surprising

---

3 *Ibid.* 46 - 7.

that a convinced Protestant like Cecil, with Court and university connections, achieved preferment. He entered the service of Hertford, now duke of Somerset and Lord Protector, in 1547 and made such a good impression that he was promoted to the post of Somerset's personal secretary in 1548. The researches of Dr M.L. Bush and Professor Dale Hoak[4] have revealed the incompetence of Somerset's government and the extent to which his policy of largely bypassing the Privy Council infuriated its members. As a result Cecil was caught up for the next five years in a complicated web of political intrigues. These involved first of all a conflict between Somerset and John Dudley, earl of Warwick, soon to be duke of Northumberland, for control of the state, and then, after Northumberland's final victory, his attempt to alter the succession to the throne - as laid down in Henry VIII's will and by act of parliament - in order to secure the accession of Lady Jane Grey, whom he married to his son Guildford Dudley. Cecil survived these dangerous events through some luck and a great deal of good judgment. After Somerset's initial fall from power in 1549 he tried to act as conciliator between him and Northumberland and after Somerset's partial rehabilitation in 1550 tried hard, and on the whole successfully, to keep on good terms with both. The extent of his skill is revealed by the fact that he managed to avoid all taint at the time of Somerset's final fall and execution in 1551. Meanwhile, his political abilities received their first full recognition when he was made a privy councillor and one

---

4 M. Bush, *The Government Policy of Protector Somerset* (1975); D.E. Hoak, *The King's Council in the Reign of Edward VI* (Cambridge, 1976).

of two secretaries of state in September 1550. The secretaries of state were the lynchpins of Tudor administration, responsible for a vast range of domestic and foreign duties. At first Cecil played himself into office fairly quietly, taking a lesser role than his experienced colleague Sir William Petre, but his abilities were soon obvious and he seemed set for a dazzling career as long as Edward VI lived. By 1553, however, it was clear that Edward was dying and Northumberland, desperate to prevent the accession of the Catholic Mary, drew up an instrument in the king's name transferring the right to the Crown to Lady Jane Grey. All the councillors were ordered to sign, but none of them anguished more over the issue than Cecil. As a believer in the supremacy of statute law he felt that he should adhere to Mary's cause. On the other hand, his Protestant faith favoured the accession of Lady Jane. Finally, on the direct orders of the king, he signed, probably the last of all the councillors to do so.

In Mary's reign he retired into private life though it was said that the Queen was willing to keep him in office if he openly accepted Catholicism. He refused such public endorsement of an ecclesiastical system which he firmly believed to be against God's word - if he had remained on the Council he would have had to take part of the responsibility for the restoration of Catholicism and its imposition on the nation - but once the old Church had been restored by lawful authority he was prepared to conform to it as a private person; he regarded that as part of his duty as a subject. He was also prepared to undertake any specific tasks which the Queen set for him, and she did indeed employ him on a couple of foreign missions. Meanwhile he continued to serve Princess Elizabeth, now heiress to the throne, as her surveyor, a post to which he had been appointed in 1550, though he had known the princess much longer.[5]

By 1558 Cecil had learned most of the lessons and developed most of the characteristics which were to stand him in good stead in his Elizabethan career. His intellectual abilities and interests were obvious during his Cambridge days and the diligence which became legendary during his later career was already evident both at Cambridge and in his years in government service between 1547 and 1553. He also showed his abilities as a conciliator during Edward's reign when he tried to mediate between the dukes of Somerset and Northumberland. His failure is perhaps less remarkable than the fact that he managed to remain on good terms with both of them. His respect for the authority of parliament, as enshrined in statute law, was very evident in the mental agonies which he went through before he could bring himself to sign the Edwardian instrument which transferred the succession from Mary to Lady Jane Grey, while his dislike of Catholicism was obvious in his behaviour during Mary's reign. Above all, perhaps, he appears as a survivor, a man who threaded his way through the secular and religious politics of the years 1547 - 58 with considerable skill. Already by 1558 he began to appear as almost an elder statesman, a figure of *gravitas*. On the other hand, as we have seen, he had been quite prepared to gamble, in the early years of his life both with his possessions

5 Burghley's role in the events of Edward VI's and Mary's reigns is discussed in Read, i, 37ff and Beckingsale, *Burghley*, 26ff.

and with his future prospects in the world; he was no
dessicated calculating machine when he fell in love with
and married Mary Cheke. So Cecil emerges in his pre-
Elizabethan career as an essentially cautious man, but
one who was capable of bold and decisive action when
he thought that the situation merited it. That latter char-
acteristic was still evident at times in his Elizabethan
ministry,[6] but the conservatism and dislike of risk-taking
which had always been a strong element in his personal-
ity, became more and more obvious during the middle
and later periods of Elizabeth's reign.

## II. QUEEN AND MINISTER

By 1558 Elizabeth had formed a fundamental judgment
of Burghley which she never changed. That judgment
was enshrined in her words to him on 20 November
1558, three days after her accession to the throne, when
she held her first Privy Council meeting. She appointed
him to the Council, made him her secretary of state, and
said to him

> I give you this charge, that you shall be of my
> Privy Council and content to take pains for
> me and my realm. This judgment I have of
> you that you will not be corrupted by any
> manner of gift and that you will be faithful to
> the state; and that, without respect of my pri-
> vate will, you will give me that counsel which

---

6 See Read, i, 117ff; W.T. MacCaffrey, *The Shaping of the Elizabethan
Regime 1558 - 1572* (1969) - henceforth MacCaffrey, i - *passim.*

you think best and, if you shall know any-
thing necessary to be declared to me of se-
crecy, you shall show it to myself alone.[7]

Throughout their long partnership, and despite its ups
and downs, she never revised that basic appraisal, and in
the very last year of his life, she acknowledged her deep
debt to the man whom she nicknamed her 'spirit' and
her continuing dependence upon him when she sent him
a cordial, accompanied by her best wishes for his recov-
ery from illness, saying that 'she did intreat heaven daily
for his longer life - else would her people, nay herself,
stand in need of cordials too.'[8] For long after his death
she wept when his name was mentioned.

Elizabeth's attitude towards Burghley was more straight-
forward than his attitude towards her, which must be
considered in the context of general sixteenth century
views on women rulers. In 1558, just before Elizabeth's
accession to the throne, John Knox published his *First
Blast of the Trumpet against the Monstrous Regiment of
Women*, in which he wrote that 'to promote a woman to
bear rule, superiority, dominion or empire above any
realm, nation or city is repugnant to nature, contumely
to God, a thing most contrary to his revealed will and
approved ordinance.'[9] These sentiments, though not, perhaps, the fiery language in which they were expressed,

---

7 Read, i, 119.

8 J. Hurstfield, *Freedom, Corruption and Government in Elizabethan
England* (1973), 106.

9 A.G.R. Smith, *The Government of Elizabethan England* (1967), 6.

were acceptable to most men of the day, and we know
that, in the early years of Elizabeth's reign, Burghley
expressed some scepticism about her capability. In 1560
he was very angry when a messenger discussed with the
Queen a dispatch from the English ambassador in France,
'being too much for a woman's knowledge.' Later in
his life, however, his attitude had completely changed.
'There was never so wise a woman born ... as Queen
Elizabeth', he stated, for she 'knew all estates and dispo-
sitions of all princes, and so expert in her own as no
councillor she had could tell her that she knew not.'[10]

If Burghley's opinion of the Queen's abilities as a person grew as the reign progressed, his conception of his
duty to her as a councillor remained constant. As God's
anointed, the divinely sanctioned sovereign of England,
she was due the allegiance which he, like all his contemporaries, acknowledged when he knelt in her presence.
In a letter to his son Robert Cecil, written in 1596, he
stated,

> I do hold, and will always, this course in such
> matters as I differ in opinion from her Maj-
> esty; as long as I may be allowed to give
> advice I will not change my opinion by af-
> firming the contrary, for that were to offend
> God, to whom I am sworn first; but as a ser-
> vant I will obey her Majesty's commandment
> and no wise contrary the same, presuming that
> she, being god's chief minister here, it shall
> be God's will to have her commandments

10 C. Haigh, *Elizabeth I* (1988), 9; Smith, *Anonymous Life*, 145 - 6.

obeyed after that I have performed my duty as a councillor.

He made the same basic points two years later in the last letter which he wrote with his own hand when he told Robert Cecil to 'serve God, by serving of the Queen, for all other service is indeed bondage to the devil.'[11]

The roots of Burghley's influence with Elizabeth can be found in the sentiments which he revealed in these two letters as well as in other qualities which he displayed, notably his fine intellect allied to a deep understanding of human nature; he recognized that it was dangerous to appear too powerful in the Queen's eyes. It was that recognition of the limits of his power, the care he took never to presume too far, that made his influence with Elizabeth all the greater. It is difficult to imagine him acting as his rival Leicester did when one of his followers was prevented by a gentleman usher from entering the Queen's privy chamber. Leicester threatened to have the usher sacked, but Elizabeth had other ideas; 'my lord', she told Leicester, 'I have wished you well but my favour is not so locked up for you that others shall not partake thereof; for I have many servants unto whom I have and will at my pleasure bequeath my favour and likewise resume the same. And if you think to rule here I will take a course to see you forthcoming. I will have here but one mistress and no master....'[12]

---

**11** J. Hurstfield and A.G.R. Smith, eds, *Elizabethan People : State and Society* (1972), 141; Read, ii, 545.

**12** Hurstfield and Smith, *Elizabethan People*, 142.

Of course, Burghley and the Queen did not always see
eye to eye on major issues and when Burghley was convinced that Elizabeth was wrong he did everything in his
power by way of pressure, exercised either directly or
indirectly on his mistress, to achieve his ends. It is worth
examining three such episodes; the Scottish crisis of 1559
- 60, the Dudley courtship and the question of the succession in the early 1560s, and the events surrounding
the execution of Mary Queen of Scots in 1587.

In the spring of 1559 there was a major Scottish revolt
against the rule of Mary of Guise, Queen Regent for her
daughter Mary Queen of Scots, then absent in France.
Cecil saw the opportunity which this provided for the
reduction of French influence in Scotland and pressed
strongly for English help for the rebels. He had to con-
vince a reluctant Elizabeth and a divided Privy Council,
but he secured financial help and then naval and military
intervention on behalf of the Scots. This was of decisive
importance in securing the success of the Scottish Refor-
mation of 1560 and the subsequent departure of French
troops from the country, but Cecil had had to resort to
threats of resignation to get his way. The whole episode
revealed that, in these early years of his Elizabethan
career, he was ready to take bold initiatives and press
ahead with them despite the Queen's doubts.[13]

It was in 1559, too, that Elizabeth's growing intimacy
with the handsome Lord Robert Dudley began to be
noticed. He was a son of John Dudley, duke of Northumberland, who had been executed early in Mary Tu-

13 Read, i, 159 - 61; MacCaffrey, i, 57ff.

12

dor's reign following his attempt to prevent her succession to the throne. Dudley already had a wife, but Cecil became increasingly afraid that the Queen was determined to marry him and that she would eventually find a way of doing so, ruining the country and bringing Cecil's own career to an end in the process. He talked once more of resignation and, in September 1560, at the height of his fears, Dudley's wife, Amy Robsart, was found dead in mysterious circumstances. Rumours multiplied, both at home and abroad, that she had been murdered. Cecil was in despair, but Elizabeth came to realise that, in the circumstances, a Dudley marriage would be politically impossible, and by the summer of 1561 the worst of the crisis was over. Elizabeth showed political realism by deciding not to marry Dudley though the latter may have taken some consolation from his elevation to the earldom of Leicester in 1564.[14]

By 1563, when parliament met with Elizabeth still unmarried, there was widespread unease among M.P.s and peers that the Queen had no generally recognised heir. She had nearly died of smallpox in 1562 and it seems likely that, if she had not survived the attack, there would have been civil war. Hence the 1563 demands in parliament that the Queen should marry and name a successor. These escalated in the next parliamentary session, in 1566, when, at one time, it looked as if there might be a complete breach over the issue between the Queen and the two houses of parliament. Cecil fully supported these demands for settling the succession and was a leading

---

**14** J.E. Neale, *Queen Elizabeth* (Penguin ed., 1960), 81ff; MacCaffrey, i, 72ff; Read, i, 198ff.

figure in the united front of Privy Council, Lords and Commons which put the most intense pressure upon the Queen to name a successor. She resisted all their efforts and Cecil was left worried and dissatisfied at the end of the session.[15]

Elizabeth's and Cecil's differences over Scotland and the succession, though serious, did not lead to a prolonged breach between the two. The circumstances surrounding the execution of Mary Queen of Scots in 1587 were different. Since her flight from Scotland to England in 1568 Mary had been involved in a variety of plots to murder Elizabeth and secure her own succession to the English throne. The climax came with her participation in the Babington plot of 1586. Privy Council, Lords and Commons united in demanding her death. Elizabeth prevaricated, first of all refusing to sign Mary's death warrant and, eventually, when she did, carefully failing to order its dispatch. It was then that Burghley intervened decisively, calling an informal meeting of privy councillors at which it was resolved to send the warrant without further reference to the Queen. As a result Mary was executed in February 1587. Burghley was banished from Court as a result of his leading role in the affair and did not regain the Queen's full confidence for several months. It was by far the most serious breach between Queen and minister during the reign and a symbol of Elizabeth's passionate feelings about a matter which concerned her so deeply, both as a woman and as a sovereign, and of Burghley's equally firm conviction

15 G.R. Elton, *The Parliament of England, 1559 - 1581* (Cambridge, 1986), 358ff.

that he must act in what he regarded as the vital interests of both his Queen and his country. There are few historians today who would deny that Burghley was right in his political judgment; there were no serious plots against Elizabeth's life after Mary's execution.[16]

Such individual examples of disagreement, though clearly of considerable significance, should not be allowed to conceal the fundamental fact that they were exceptions to the general harmony which prevailed between Queen and minister. Elizabeth and Burghley lived in the 'post-revolutionary' England of the later 16th century. Both accepted the fundamentals of the constitutional and religious changes of the reigns of Henry VIII and Edward VI but both believed that once Mary's counter-revolution of 1553 - 8 had been undone then the country needed as much domestic and foreign peace and stability as it could get. In specific instances they differed about the best way to secure these aims, but on the aims themselves they were agreed; that was the major reason for both the length and the strength of their partnership.

That partnership lasted for forty years and during that time Burghley's ministerial career went through three major phases, covering the years 1558 to 1572, 1572 to 1585, and 1585 until his death in 1598. During these years he held three great offices of state; he was principal secretary of state between 1558 and 1572, Master of the Court of Wards from 1561 until 1598, and Lord Treasurer from 1572 until 1598. The secretaryship had

---

16 A.G.R. Smith, *The Last Years of Mary Queen of Scots* (1990), 16ff.

developed greatly during Thomas Cromwell's ministry between 1532 and 1540 and, although its status declined under his lesser successors, Cecil raised its political importance to Cromwellian heights during his tenure of the post. As the Queen's principal adviser he was concerned with all aspects of foreign and domestic policy and the secretaryship, with its very flexible duties, was an ideal vehicle for his purposes. His son, Robert Cecil, who himself held the secretaryship between 1596 and 1612, remarked that, unlike other officials, who had clearly defined duties, 'to the secretary, out of a confidence and singular affection, there is liberty to negotiate at discretion at home and abroad ... all matters of speech and intelligence.[17]

During Burghley's tenure of the office he demonstrated his willingness to take the lead in bold ventures. One of these was the Scottish episode of 1559 - 60,[18] another was the Spanish treasure affair in 1568 - 9. In 1567 the duke of Alba, Spain's greatest soldier, arrived with an army in the Netherlands in order to put down the revolt there. The following year a fleet was dispatched by Spain to the Netherlands carrying funds, borrowed in Genoa, for the payment of Alba's troops. Some of the ships took refuge in ports in Devon and Cornwall to escape the attention of Protestant pirates. The English government learnt that the money which they carried would not be the legal property of the Spanish govern-

17 F.M.G. Evans, *The Principal Secretary of State* (Manchester, 1923), 59. Evans's book is still the best study of the secretary's office.

18 See above, 11.

ment until it arrived in the Netherlands, so, in December 1568, on the grounds that it still belonged to Genoese financiers, Burghley and the Queen decided to borrow it themselves. Professor MacCaffrey has demonstrated beyond much doubt[19] that it was Burghley who took the lead in this decision to challenge the great west European power of the day. His reasons are still not altogether clear,[20] but whatever they were the incident was a prelude to a great crisis both for Elizabeth's government and for him personally. In 1569 there was a plot to marry Mary Queen of Scots to Thomas Howard, duke of Norfolk, England's premier nobleman; a Leicester-Norfolk intrigue to overthrow Cecil; and the revolt of the northern earls, a rising by conservative noblemen which was due to a variety of causes but certainly included in its aims both the removal of Cecil and the restoration of Catholicism. All three of these challenges to Elizabeth's authority were defeated, but they were followed in 1570 by the Papal bull *regnans in excelsis*, declaring her deposed, and, in 1571, by the Ridolphi plot, a Catholic conspiracy which involved both Spain and the duke of Norfolk and aimed at her overthrow and the accession of Mary. After the discovery of the plot Norfolk was executed in 1572 and in the same year England signed a defensive alliance with France, the traditional national enemy.[21] This 'diplomatic revolution' of 1572 marked the beginning of a calmer period in English domestic and foreign affairs.

---

**19** MacCaffrey, i, 189ff.

**20** But see MacCaffrey's speculations, i, 192 - 4.

**21** MacCaffrey, i, 199ff; Read, i, 431ff; ii, 17ff.

The years 1558 until 1572, the first phase of Burghley's Elizabethan career, saw, therefore, his firm establishment as the Queen's chief adviser. He defended his position with great skill during the dramatic events of 1568 - 9, but the key to his survival during these conflicts was the Queen's trust. She emphasized her confidence in him when she raised him to the peerage in 1571 and, in 1572, appointed him to the great office of Lord Treasurer, left vacant by the death of the aged marquess of Winchester. As for Leicester, he retained Elizabeth's deep affection, perhaps even her love, but the events of 1568 to 1572 revealed the limits of his political power. In 1572, in Professor MacCaffrey's words, 'Burghley ... stood pre-eminent.'[22]

The second phase of Burghley's Elizabethan ministry, the period between his appointment as Lord Treasurer and the outbreak of war with Spain in 1585, has attracted different verdicts from Professors Conyers Read and MacCaffrey. Read argued that the change of office relieved him of 'the crushing load of detailed administration ...; though he assumed responsibility for the national finances, he was primarily hereafter a counsellor.' MacCaffrey on the other hand has stated that during these years he was 'the dynamo which kept the routine business of government running smoothly and effectively' and elaborates the point by indicating the vast range of business with which he dealt.[23] It is MacCaffrey's rather

---

22 MacCaffrey, i, 295.

23 Read, ii, 85; W.T. MacCaffrey, *Queen Elizabeth and the Making of Policy 1572 - 1588* (Princeton, 1981) - henceforth MacCaffrey, ii - 456.

18

than Read's verdict which carries conviction, especially when we note Michael Hickes's description of the immense quantities of work which Burghley continued to undertake from the 1570s onwards.[24] On the other hand, MacCaffrey is less convincing when he argues that, in the years after 1572, it is 'very difficult to ascertain what he counselled. When we do have his views, they meticulously add up pros and cons so as to leave the scale in perfect balance.'[25] It is true that Burghley did weigh up the advantages and disadvantages of any particular line of action - and often wrote his thoughts down - but it is wrong to imply that he always sat on the fence when it came to important decisions. It seems certain that he firmly supported the final crucial decision in 1585 to send English troops to the Netherlands to aid the rebels there in their struggle against Spain, and equally clear that in 1587 he was the driving force in the decision to send off Mary Queen of Scots' execution warrant without Elizabeth's explicit approval.[26] He may have been more cautious in the second and third phases of his ministry than he was in the first, but he was still capable of decisive action when he was sure that the situation warranted it.

The third and final phase of his ministry began with the outbreak of war with Spain in 1585. From then on he had to cope with the immense financial and administra-

---

24 See below, 21, 27.

25 MacCaffrey, ii, 455 - 6.

26 R.B. Wernham, *The Making of Elizabethan Foreign Policy 1558 - 1603* (Berkeley, California, 1980), 71 - 2.

tive burdens of the war - the Privy Council registers are
full of details which indicate the extent of these burdens
- and he had to do so at a time when he was waging
another, and losing, battle against increasing age and ill
health. No wonder contemporaries marvelled at his remarkable endurance! During these years too he lost the
help of many of the most prominent members of the
Privy Council. Leicester died in 1588; Sir Walter
Mildmay, a notable financial expert, in 1589; Sir Francis
Walsingham, secretary of state and spymaster, in 1590;
Ambrose Dudley, earl of Warwick, Leicester's brother,
also in 1590; and Sir Christopher Hatton, a capable poli-
tician as well as a favourite of the Queen, in 1591. At
least Burghley had increasing help from his able younger
son, Robert Cecil, who was knighted in 1591 and appointed to the Privy Council in the same year. The
secretaryship had been left vacant after Walsingham's
death, when Burghley resumed the responsibilities of the
office. During the following years he handed over more
and more of the duties to his son until, in 1596, Elizabeth recognised what was virtually a *fait accompli* when
she formally appointed Robert to the secretaryship. The
1590s also revealed the growing political ambitions of
Elizabeth's last favourite, Leicester's stepson, Robert
Devereux, earl of Essex, and thus foreshadowed the open
struggle for power in the state between Essex and Robert
Cecil, which reached its climax, after Burghley's death,
between 1598 and 1601.[27]

These different phases of Burghley's career should re-

---

27 J. Hurstfield, 'The Succession Struggle in Late Elizabethan England',
*Elizabethan Government and Society, Essays presented to Sir John
Neale*, eds. S.T. Bindoff, J. Hurstfield, C.H. Williams (1961), 369ff.

mind us of truths about the Elizabethan period which historians can too easily forget. Its great length meant that the problems which the Queen and her ministers faced changed substantially during the reign and also that most of the principal actors in the drama - most notably of all the Queen and Burghley - who had been young or middle aged at the start, were old as it drew towards its end. As she aged the Queen's instinctive conservatism and reluctance to take decisions intensified, and these characteristics both fed and were fed by the conservatism and tortured doubts of her principal minister. Burghley could still be a good deal more decisive than his mistress - witness his bold actions in 1587 - but the increasingly laborious weighing up of pros and cons to which MacCaffrey referred was an indication that, as he grew old, Burghley became ever more capable of seeing both sides of a question.

## III. PATRONAGE

The confidence which the Queen placed in Burghley was reflected in the fact that she entrusted him with a larger share of her patronage than any other man.[28] Most suitors for royal favour had no direct contact with or access to the sovereign and had to pursue their claims

---

28 For discussions of the patronage system see J.E. Neale, 'The Elizabethan Political Scene', *Essays in Elizabethan History* (1958), 59 - 84; W.T. MacCaffrey, 'Place and Patronage in Elizabethan Politics', *Elizabethan Government and Society*, 95 - 126; Smith, *The Government of Elizabethan England*, chapter 5; A.G.R. Smith, *The Emergence of a Nation State* (1984), chapter 14; *Servant of the Cecils : the Life of Sir Michael Hickes* (1977), chapter 3; P. Williams, *The Tudor Regime* (Oxford, 1979), chapter 3.

21

through intermediaries. Some did so by letter, while others thronged the court trying to persuade influential ministers or favourites to take up their cause. Privy councillors were both recipients and distributors of patronage. They held their own positions and influence through royal favour, and, in their turn, used that influence to advance the suits of others. Part of Burghley's patronage derived from his offices of Master of the Wards and Lord Treasurer, which gave him the right to appoint to many lesser posts, but much of it symbolised the fact that he was Elizabeth's chief adviser. The extent of his patronage imposed a very heavy burden of work on him. Hickes reported that Burghley

> drew upon him such multitudes of suits as was incredible but to us that saw it, for ... there was not a day ... wherein he received not threescore, fourscore and an hundred petitions, which he commonly read that night and gave every man answer the next morning. ... But after he grew impotent and weak ... he devised a new way ..., that, by age and infirmities being forced to keep his chamber and sometimes his bed, he took order that poor suitors should send in their petitions sealed up, whereby the poorest man's bill came to him as soon as the rich. Upon every petition he caused his answer to be written on the back side and subscribed it with his own name, or else they had his letter or other answer as the cause required.[29]

29 Smith, *Anonymous Life*, 66 - 8.

Burghley's role in the distribution of patronage brought him wealth. He certainly took gifts. Professor Hurstfield revealed that during the last two and a half years of his life he received at least £3,000 from suitors for wardships at a time when his salary as Master of the Court of Wards was only £133 a year. At his death his gold and silver plate, much of which probably came from gifts made by clients, was worth at least £14,000.[30] Especially revealing is Burghley's relations with the merchant, financier and entrepreneur Thomas Smith. Through his association with the collection of customs dues Smith became known as Customer Smith and acquired considerable profits. In 1589 it was estimated that he had made £50,000 over the previous 19 years from his farm of the duties on goods imported at London and there is a great deal of evidence that he gave Burghley up to £2,000 in order to secure his customs privileges.[31] These examples help to explain the sources of Burghley's very considerable wealth. He invested his profits of office in lands and buildings. He built (or rebuilt) three splendid residences, Cecil House, on the north side of the Strand, between London and Westminster; Burghley House in Northamptonshire; and Theobalds in Hertfordshire. The last two, especially, were extremely impressive. Burghley House, a huge edifice, is today one of the most imposing of all surviving Elizabethan houses and Theobalds, now no longer standing, was the greatest of all his mansions

---

30 J. Hurstfield, *The Queen's Wards* (1958), 266ff; Williams, *The Tudor Regime*, 96.

31 H.A. Lloyd, 'Camden, Carmarden and the Customs', *English Historical Review*, lxxxv (1970), 776 - 87. I would like to thank my colleague Dr Brian Dietz for information on this point.

and one of the wonders of the age. Its enormous size - it was perhaps the largest secular building in England after Whitehall and Hampton Court palaces when it was completed in 1585 - can be partly explained by Burghley's determination to provide a fitting setting for the Queen during her numerous visits there. She came twelve times altogether and each visit cost him a small fortune. All his houses were noted for their splendid interiors but Theobalds, as the awestruck reports of visitors make clear, had especially impressive internal decorations.[32] He also acquired a huge landed estate scattered across the home counties and the east midlands and running as far north as Yorkshire. At his death in 1598 this passed to his sons Thomas and Robert. The former, as elder son, obtained the bulk of the inheritance and in 1602 had a rental of well over £5,000 *per annum*, making him one of the five richest peers in England. Robert's lands probably brought him about £1,800 a year.[33] It was on these inheritances that the present day marquessates of Exeter and Salisbury were built.

Burghley's diversion of the private wealth of suitors into his own pockets would have made him a corrupt man by 20th century British standards, but in 16th century England, when salaries were small, the practice of giving and taking gratuities was generally accepted. In 16th century terms a man's probity has to be judged not by whether or not he took gifts - everybody did - but by other criteria. One of these is the relationship between a

---

32 Smith, *Servant of the Cecils*, 36.

33 L. Stone, *Family and Fortune* (Oxford, 1973), 3 - 4; *The Crisis of the Aristocracy* (Oxford, 1965), 760.

24

man's gains and the chances open to him. Here Burghley has generally come out well in the judgments of historians. Sir John Neale, for example, in his famous lecture on 'the Elizabethan Political Scene' argued that, although Burghley took gratuities, 'others were in the game, much more deeply in relation to their opportunities.'[34] We should remember, however, that the whole question of gratuities is complicated by the nature of the surviving evidence. The Cecil papers, preserved at Hatfield House and in the British Library, contain material about Burghley's and Robert Cecil's roles in the workings of the patronage system which is not available in the same quantity for any other Elizabethan statesman, and from that material it is easy to conclude that Robert Cecil took many more gifts at the end of the 16th century than his father had done in earlier years. Professor Hurstfield, however, has argued that 'Robert Cecil was a cynic and discussed with his intimates the gifts he took; and some of these discussions have survived among his papers. His father was a hypocrite and he kept his thoughts very much to himself.'[35] We do not have to agree entirely with that verdict to appreciate the complexities of the issue. It is perhaps best to conclude that Burghley certainly took gratuities and gifts which helped him to build up a great fortune but that it is almost impossible to judge whether he took more or less of such *douceurs* than his contemporaries.

34 J.E. Neale, 'The Elizabethan Political Scene', *Essays in Elizabethan History*, 65.

35 J. Hurstfield, 'Political Corruption in Modern England : the historian's problem, *Freedom, Corruption and Government*, 142.

If the taking of gratuities was generally accepted in the 16th century, some practices were clearly regarded as corrupt. One of these, then as now, was the perversion of justice for personal ends. Here a verdict on Burghley is relatively easy to establish. Contemporaries lauded his reputation as a judge. Michael Hickes stated that 'in causes depending before him in justice he regarded neither friend nor enemy, for he would be neither partial to the one nor inclining to revenge or wrong the other.' John Clapham, another member of his household, echoed these sentiments when he wrote that Burghley's presence in court was much desired by suitors who wanted to have their cases 'heard only before him'.[36] Modern research has confirmed these views. Hurstfield has established that, as a judge in the Court of Wards, Burghley was both patient and honest and Read has pointed out that in many cases in the Court of Exchequer litigants asked for their hearing to be postponed until Burghley himself could preside.[37]

Another practice which was certainly regarded as corrupt was using office or influence to advance, for fiscal or other personal advantage, blatantly unworthy men who would be inadequate as servants of the state or, alternatively, hindering the advancement of men of ability in order to preserve one's own position or influence. Burghley was certainly accused by contemporaries of hindering the promotion of able men. Thomas Wilson, author and intelligencer, repeated this charge in 1601 when he noted

---

36 Smith, *Anonymous Life*, 79; E.P. and C. Read, eds, *Elizabeth of England* (Philadelphia, 1951), 81.

37 Hurstfield, *The Queen's Wards*, 216, 269 - 71; Read ii, 83.

complaints that Burghley had been 'like an aged tree that lets none grow which near him planted be.'[38] Such accusations were certainly exaggerated. Even if Burghley had wanted to surround himself and the Queen with mediocrities - and there is no real evidence that he did - he would almost certainly have failed. He had great influence with Elizabeth but it was she who made the final decisions in appointments to the highest offices of state and the names of the able privy councillors who served her - names like Nicholas Bacon, Walsingham, Hatton and Egerton - reveal that she was generally a good judge of men.

The balance of the evidence, then, suggests that Burghley was not a corrupt man by 16th century standards. He did make great profits from office, but these must be related to his even greater opportunities. He was a diligent and impartial judge, and there is no significant evidence that he attempted to surround the queen with mediocrities in order to bolster his own position.

## IV. CHURCH AND STATE

In discussing Burghley's role in the patronage system we have noted the hordes of suitors who pursued him. Their numbers are one indication of the pressures to which he was subjected. His devotion to duty ensured that he seldom rested. He had 'an infinite capacity for

---

38 Smith, *Anonymous Life*, 101; T. Wilson, 'The State of England in 1600', ed. F.J. Fisher, *Camden Miscellany*, xvi (1936), 42.

taking pains'[39] in affairs of state.  Hickes, commenting on his diligence, stated that his 'labour and care' in the Queen's service 'was so incessant and his study so great as, in cases of necessity, he cared neither for meat, sleep or rest, till his business was brought to some end. ... His industry ... caused all his friends to pity him and his very servants to admire him.'[40] The overwhelming mass of state papers which bear marks of his personal attention provide confirmation of that judgment and reflect his reluctance to delegate even fairly routine tasks. In the last years of his life he still had only a small personal secretariat to help him with his multifarious duties.[41] His capacity for work was all the more remarkable because of his frequent illnesses.  From the age of thirty-three onwards he was plagued by attacks of gout and among his papers in the British Library are letters to him from all parts of Europe, offering him a wide variety of remedies, including 'medicated slippers', an alchemical tincture of gold, and 'oil of stag's blood'.  We do not know how many of these nostrums he tried, but he continued to suffer from increasingly frequent, prolonged and painful attacks of the disease.[42]

---

**39** J. Hurstfield, 'Burghley : William Cecil, 1520 - 1598', *History Today*, 6 (1956), 798.

**40** Smith, *Anonymous Life*, 59

**41** A.G.R. Smith, 'The Secretariats of the Cecils, circa 1580 - 1612', *English Historical Review*, lxxxiii (1968), 481 - 504.

**42** W.S.C. Copeman, 'The Gout of William Cecil, First Lord Burghley', *Medical History*, i (1957), 262 - 4. Burghley's constant ill health during the last decade of his life is detailed in Read, ii, 477 - 546.

It was fortunate indeed for England that Burghley had such immense powers of work throughout his long life. Without them he would have had no chance of performing effectively the very many duties which the Queen asked him to undertake. This was not only because of the range of these duties - in his capacity as the Queen's chief adviser he might be expected to deal with virtually any matter of state or problem of administration - but also because he was expected to combine the work of minister and civil servant; in the 16th century there was not the distinction between these two roles which exists today.

In the Elizabethan period the general aims of government were limited.[43] The main objectives were to preserve peace at home, defend the realm against foreign threats, and raise enough money to achieve these primary tasks. Also important was an obligation to take an interest in the welfare of the poorer sections of the population, an obligation rooted not only in the need to preserve order - the discontented poor might riot - but also in Christian and humanistic teaching about the need to care for the less fortunate members of the community. All this amounted, in a general sense, to the achievement and maintenance of stability. Burghley and other Elizabethan ministers used a variety of methods to try and achieve these ends. Among the most important were intelligence, propaganda, and efficient administration.

While he was secretary Burghley created an effective

---

43 These aims are discussed in A.G.R. Smith, *Tudor Government* (Historical Association, New Appreciations in History, 20, 1990).

intelligence network both at home and abroad. The information he obtained from his spies was not only valuable in countering threats to English interests, it also helped his growing reputation for omniscience. Other councillors also had their informants, but only Walsingham, in the 1570s and 1580s, was able to build up an intelligence network which surpassed Burghley's in efficiency.[44] Burghley was also Elizabeth's director of propaganda. He encouraged the leaders of the Elizabethan church and state to defend the regime in writings as well as in their actions and himself wrote and published propagandist works. The most important was *The Execution of Justice in England*, published in 1583, the official justification of the treatment of Catholic missionaries in England.[45] Burghley's work on the Privy Council illustrates his concern for effective administration. The Council was the central administrative institution of the realm and it superintended the government of England with great diligence, concerning itself with everything that went on in the country. Burghley was a regular attender in the very last years of his life, just as he had been in the first years of Elizabeth's reign. His attention to the routine business of the Council between 1558 and 1598 is one of the most striking illustrations of his devoted service to the state.[46]

---

44 C. Read, *Mr Secretary Walsingham and the Policy of Queen Elizabeth*, 3 vols (Oxford, 1925).

45 C. Read, 'William Cecil and Elizabethan Public Relations', *Elizabethan Government and Society*, 21ff.

46 For the Privy Council and Burghley's role in it, Smith, *The Government of Elizabethan England*, chapter 2.

When Burghley and the Queen, at the beginning of the reign, began the task of creating peace and stability in England, one of their foremost concerns was the settlement of the Church. In the 16th century Church and state were in theory co-terminous, each including the whole population. Indeed, the work of the Church, the salvation of men's souls, was in principle more important than that of the state, the government of men's bodies. The Elizabethan Church settlement, therefore, which renewed the English breach with Rome and provided a form of worship for the Church of England, was of crucial importance. Sir John Neale believed that the 1559 settlement represented a compromise between the views of a relatively radical House of Commons and a relatively conservative Queen, but recent research, especially that of Professor Jones, has indicated convincingly that the settlement was a triumph for the Queen and Burghley. The acts of Supremacy and Uniformity represented a victory for them, in alliance with the Commons, against a much more conservative House of Lords.[47] During the rest of the reign they faced two major challenges to their newly established Church, from the Catholics and the Puritans.

Burghley's attitude to the Catholics, enshrined in *The Execution of Justice in England*, was an affirmation of his belief in an English nation state subject to no exter-

---

47 J.E. Neale, 'The Elizabethan Acts of Supremacy and Uniformity', *English Historical Review*, lxv (1950), 304 - 32; *Elizabeth I and her Parliaments*, volume i, 51ff; N. Jones, *Faith by Statute : Parliament and the Settlement of Religion, 1559* (1982); W.S. Hudson, *The Cambridge Connection and the Elizabethan Settlement of 1559* (Durham, North Carolina, 1980).

nal authority. That nation state had been created by Henry VIII and Thomas Cromwell, renounced by Mary and recreated by Elizabeth and himself. The Catholics, because they recognised the authority of a foreign ruler, the Pope, could not accept the basis of the Elizabethan state and the harsh legislation directed against them in the later years of the reign was fully justified, in Burghley's eyes, for that reason alone. The 180 Catholics, 120 of them priests, who were executed between 1581 and 1603 were in his eyes traitors to their country just as in their own and in foreign Catholic eyes they were martyrs for their faith. Both sides were right. At a time when politics and religion were inextricably intertwined and Popes claimed the right to depose heretical rulers Catholics who suffered death were both traitors and martyrs.[48]

Unlike the Catholic threat, which was an attack on the Church of England from outside, the Puritan threat came from within.[49] Definition of the term Puritan has caused much debate among historians, but, broadly speaking, Puritans can be seen as those 'hotter' Protestants who wished to purge the Church of remaining Popish abuses. They differed among themselves as to just what these abuses were and there is no suggestion that Burghley had any sympathy for those more extreme Puritans, the Presbyterians, who numbered bishops among the 'Popish relics' and who achieved some influence in the Church during the 1570s and 1580s. On the other hand, he has been seen as the patron of the more moderate Puritanism

48 Smith, *The Emergence of a Nation State*, 152.

49 By far the best discussion of Elizabethan Puritanism is P. Collinson, *The Elizabethan Puritan Movement* (1967).

which accepted bishops but stressed the role of the Bible, predestinarian theology, preaching, and a learned ministry in the life of the Church. He certainly employed men with strong Puritan beliefs in his household - his secretaries Skinner and Hickes are examples[50] - but it has been pointed out that there was not the slightest trace of Puritan inclinations in the two collections of precepts, some of them containing worthy religious sentiments, which he drew up for his sons. More important, there is no trace at all of Puritan ideas in his will; no references to predestination or the elect, no bequests to maintain Godly preachers. Moreover, he chose as one of the overseers of the will that bane of the Puritans, Archbishop Whitgift.[51] Burghley, in fact, appears to have been a sincerely devout man of moderate views who firmly believed that the clergy should be kept in their places. It is now often stressed that the 16th and early 17th centuries were a period in which the laity triumphed over the clergy in the running of the Church. That was a development which Burghley strongly supported and indeed to which he made a significant contribution. He was one of the great Erastians of the period.

If one of Burghley's ideals was a Church subordinated to the state, another was a peaceful and stable realm which recognized and upheld the interests of the 'political nation', those gentlemen and prosperous townsmen who took an intelligent interest in the country's affairs

---

50 Smith, *Servant of the Cecils*, 21 - 2.

51 J. Hurstfield, 'Church and State, the task of the Cecils', *Freedom, Corruption and Government*, 81ff; L.B. Wright, ed., *Advice to a Son* (New York, 1962); Public Record Office Prob 1/3.

and whose co-operation, in the absence of an effective police force, a standing army, and a substantial paid bureaucracy in the localities was essential for the effective administration of England. Sir Geoffrey Elton has shown how the ambitions of these men and thus the interests of the state were catered for in three 'points of contact' between the Crown and the political nation which helped to ensure the smooth working of Tudor government.[52]

One of these was the Privy Council and we have already noted Burghley's vital role in the work of that body which was, more than any other institution, responsible for the relatively efficient administration of the Elizabethan realm. Another was the Court, where contending interests, as represented by different councillors and favourites, competed for the Queen's attention. There is little doubt that, during his forty year ministry, Burghley obtained more of that attention and hence more benefits from her than any of her other advisers. It is clear, therefore, that he was the most important figure after the Queen in the workings of both the Privy Council and the Court. He was also the prime manager of the third point of contact, parliament.

Sir John Neale in his famous study, published in the 1950s, concentrated on the great, dramatic events of Elizabethan parliamentary history.[53] He stressed the basic loy-

---

52 G.R. Elton, 'Tudor Government, the points of contact : I. Parliament, II. The Council, III. The Court, *Studies in Tudor and Stuart Politics and Government*, iii (Cambridge, 1983), 3 - 57.

53 J.E. Neale, *Elizabeth I and her Parliaments*, 2 vols (1953, 1957).

alty of M.P.s to the Queen, but his work, in its details, was essentially a story of struggles between Elizabeth and successive Houses of Commons which often opposed her over major issues concerning religion, the succession to the throne, free speech, and the royal prerogative. Since Neale's work a number of revisionist historians, led by Elton and Professor Michael Graves, have presented a very different picture, stressing that parliaments should be viewed as part of the government machine and emphasising the amount of co-operation which took place between Crown, Lords and Commons, the three elements in the parliamentary trinity. The revisionists admit, of course, that conflicts did take place, but regard these as part of the normal give and take of parliamentary proceedings, and stress instead the success of the parliaments in passing large quantities of legislation, including subsidy bills, in almost all the Elizabethan parliaments.[54] In this revised picture, which is rapidly acquiring the status of a new orthodoxy, Burghley appears as the greatest parliamentary manager of the later 16th century, guiding proceedings first of all from the House of Commons and then, from 1571 onwards, from the House of Lords. He was assisted by privy councillors and 'men of business' in the Commons, but his own role was crucial. His appreciation of the need for careful management of both Lords and Commons in the Crown's interest was reflected in his own regular attendance in parliament and in his diligence in its routine business. Even in 1597, the penultimate year of his life, he was

54 G.R. Elton, *The Parliament of England 1559 - 1581* (Cambridge, 1986); M.A.R. Graves, *The Tudor Parliaments*, 1485 - 1603 (1985); *Elizabethan Parliaments, 1559 - 1601* (1987).

present at 66% of the sittings of the Lords and a member of 19 out of 33 recorded committees and conferences which dealt with a wide variety of subjects. He remained, to quote Professor Graves, 'the devoted royal servant within parliament as much as in Council and Court.'[55]

Elizabethan parliamentary history, therefore, provides excellent illustrations of Burghley's powers of work and of his talents in the management of men. Readers of Neale's two volumes are likely to be struck by the Queen's skill in touching the hearts and minds of M.P.s and peers. Readers of Graves and Elton are more likely to be struck by the managerial abilities of Lord Burghley.

The subsidy acts, passed by almost all Elizabethan parliaments, were in response to government requests for money, usually for the preservation of England's security against real or potential foreign threats. After 1585 they reflected the war which broke out in that year between England and Spain following the dispatch of English forces to the Netherlands to aid the Dutch rebels there. English foreign policy was ultimately in the hands of the Queen who made or approved all important decisions. Sometimes she consulted the full Council, more often individual ministers. Much of the detailed work connected with foreign policy was done by the principal secretary - he, for example, drafted the routine correspondence with ambassadors and other agents abroad - and Cecil, when he was secretary between 1558 and 1572, was undoubtedly her principal adviser and executor in foreign affairs. After 1573, when Walsingham

---

55 Graves, *Tudor Parliaments*, 137 - 8.

36

took over the secretaryship, she still regularly consulted
Cecil, now Lord Burghley, on matters of foreign as well
as domestic policy. After Walsingham's death, when
Burghley took responsibility for the secretaryship once
again, he was often helped by other councillors such as
Hatton, Buckhurst and Robert Cecil.[56]

The basis of Elizabethan foreign policy was a determination to assert English independence vis à vis the two
leading west European continental powers of the period,
France and Spain, while at the same time preserving
English security and, if at all possible, keeping out of
war. The Queen and Burghley were united in these aims
and, in a bellicose era, their commitment to peace was
especially remarkable. Hickes, in his biography of
Burghley, quoted two of the latter's sayings which con-
firm the point. 'War is soon kindled, but peace very
hardly procured' and 'a realm gaineth more by one years
peace than by ten years war'.[57] In the precepts which he
wrote for Robert Cecil about 1584 Burghley made the
point again, in another way, when he stated that a committed warrior 'can hardly be an honest man or a good
Christian, for war is of itself unjust, unless the good
cause may make it just'.[58] Of course, Burghley was pre-

---

56 Elizabethan foreign policy and Burghley's role in it can best be
followed in R.B. Wernham, *The Making of Elizabethan Foreign
Policy 1558 - 1603*; *Before the Armada, 1485 - 1588* (1966); *After
the Armada, 1588 - 1595* (Oxford, 1984). See also MacCaffrey, i,
ii.

57 Smith, *Anonymous Life*, 144.

58 L.B. Wright, ed., *Advice to a Son*, 11.

pared to go to war when he felt that the overwhelming national interest demanded it - that made a war 'just' in his eyes. That attitude can be seen very clearly in the Scottish crisis of 1559 - 60, when he pressed for the dispatch of English forces to aid the rebels. It can be seen again in 1585, when he accepted the need to send English forces to the Netherlands to help the Dutch rebels in their struggle against Spain. The early 1580s saw significant changes in the balance of power in western Europe, all of them in Spain's favour, and he realized that, without English intervention, Philip II might soon be master of the whole of western Europe, an intolerable threat to English security. He went into the struggle, however, as a very reluctant warrior indeed. During the 1570s and early 1580s when a group of councillors, headed by Leicester and Walsingham, favoured a more interventionist policy in the Netherlands, their advice was resisted by Burghley and the Queen. Even in 1585 the decision to go to war caused Elizabeth and Burghley great anguish, but they realized that, by then, it could no longer be avoided.

The wisdom of their policy has been questioned by Professor Wilson, who believes that they should have intervened much earlier in the Netherlands melting pot, before the division between its northern and southern parts had crystallized; the southern provinces had been reconciled with Philip II in 1579.[59] His arguments have a superficial attraction, but there is much to be said on the other side. Above all, perhaps, it should be pointed out

---

59 C. Wilson, *Queen Elizabeth and the Revolt of the Netherlands* (1970).

that the cost of such intervention in the 1570s would have been enormous (as it was to be in the 1580s). One of the reasons for Elizabeth's success in both foreign and domestic affairs was her solvency, and Burghley and she saw clearly that this depended on keeping out of expensive foreign adventures for as long as they possibly could. By 1585 it was plain that the money would have to be found, but that seems a poor reason for arguing that it should have been found in the much more balanced international situation of the 1570s, when the huge growth of Spanish power in the early 1580s could hardly have been foreseen. By the end of the reign Spanish power had been contained - it no longer threatened to dominate the entire western part of the European continent -and the English intervention in the Netherlands and later, in the 1590s, in the French civil war, was crucially important in achieving that outcome. In 1603 England was much more secure than she had been in either 1558 or 1585. That is surely a vindication of Elizabeth's and Burghley's foreign policy. They would certainly have regarded it as such.

If the foreign policy of Elizabeth's government was designed primarily to achieve the security of England, that aim could also be seen in the government's social and economic policies. Here, too, Burghley was a crucial figure, but the old idea that he should be seen as a master planner of the Elizabethan economy[60] cannot be accepted. Almost all the economic statutes of the reign contain exemptions from their provisions for important

---

60 W.R. Cunningham, *Growth of English Industry and Commerce : Modern Times* (Cambridge, 1903), i, 53.

vested interests and Burghley's economic policy is best seen as a series of specific reactions to specific problems.[61] What does give it some coherence is that, in responding to problems, he naturally took account of his *general* aims in government, most notably the defence of the realm and the raising of revenue. These objectives were the inspiration behind his 'economic nationalism', his efforts to encourage old industries and develop new ones, and his granting of monopolies, which brought profit both to the government and to himself.[62]

The profits which monopolies brought to the Crown were very welcome at a time when Elizabeth and her government were determined to preserve English solvency. Burghley was made Lord Treasurer in 1572. He was the obvious choice for the post. He had been interested in financial affairs since the reign of Edward VI and had been closely associated with Winchester during the latter's Lord Treasurership between 1550 and 1572. After 1572 he continued Winchester's policy of economy, making cuts in the expenditure of government departments and saving up to £100,000 a year from the ordinary (i.e. regular) revenues. These surpluses created a war chest which was soon exhausted after the outbreak of war with Spain in 1585 and in the later years of the reign Elizabeth and he had to sell Crown lands and ask for more and more parliamentary taxation in order to meet the growing costs of war at sea, on the continent of Europe, and in Ireland. At the time of Elizabeth's death, however, the Crown's debt was still relatively limited,

---

61 Smith, *The Government of Elizabethan England*, chapter 6.

62 J. Thirsk, *Economic Policy and Projects* (Oxford, 1978).

not more than £350,000 - a considerable achievement in the circumstances.[63]

This seems a remarkable success story and historians have heaped praise on Elizabeth's and Burghley's financial management. Neale wrote that finance was 'the essence of Elizabeth's [success] story' and Dietz described Burghley as 'the greatest Lord Treasurer'.[64] These are tempting verdicts but before we accept them we should look at what happened to revenue from the Crown lands, from customs, from wardship, and from the principal source of parliamentary supply, the subsidy.[65] Improved methods of estate management led to a significant rise in the revenues of the Crown lands under Mary, but during Elizabeth's reign land revenues only increased from about £78,000 to about £100,000 a year, an increase of between a third and a quarter at a time when food prices and the revenues of private landlords were both rising much more quickly. Customs revenues had been boosted by a Marian reform of 1558 to £83,000 a year at the beginning of Elizabeth's reign but in 1603 they averaged

---

63 The standard financial history is still F.C. Dietz, *English Public Finance 1558 - 1641* (2nd ed., 1964). On Burghley see 30ff. For the debt in 1603, Smith, *The Government of Elizabethan England*, 8 - 9.

64 J.E. Neale, *Queen Elizabeth*, 288; Dietz, *English Public Finance*, 85.

65 For what follows, A.G.R. Smith, *The Emergence of a Nation State*, 83, 118 - 9; T.S. Willan, ed., *A Tudor Book of Rates* (Manchester, 1923); J. Guy, *Tudor England*, 382 - 3; H. Miller, 'Subsidy assessments of the peerage in the 16th century', *Bulletin of the Institute of Historical Research*, 28 (1955), 22.

only about £96,000 *per annum*. That was a poor performance at a time of rapid inflation and it can be explained by the fact that the valuations of goods in Mary's
Book of Rates, which had been fairly realistic at the
time of its issue, were not increased during Elizabeth's
reign and soon fell out of line with the true values of the
commodities. The history of the feudal dues which were
collected by the Court of Wards tells an even more dis-
mal story. Burghley was Master of the Court from 1561
until 1598 and the income from wardship was actually
higher, even in nominal terms, at the beginning of his
mastership, when it stood at £18,000 *per annum*, than it
was at the end, when it had fallen to less than £15,000 a
year. If allowance is made for inflation the fall in real
terms was a very considerable one. The yield of a subsidy, the principal parliamentary tax, was about £140,000
at the beginning of Elizabeth's reign, but only about
£80,000 at the end. This was due to a combination of
static tax assessments and widespread evasion, and
Burghley himself set a very bad example. Even after he
was raised to the peerage in 1571 he assessed himself at
only £133 a year for the rest of the reign, a ludicrous
undervaluation when his landed income alone, at the end
of his life, was probably in the region of £7,000 *per
annum*.

This is fiscal conservatism with a vengeance. Was it the
conservatism of inertia or was it conservatism with a
purpose, the preservation of political and social stability
through limiting the burden of taxation on the landed
classes? Whichever it was, it accustomed the political
nation to paying low taxes. When they were asked to
pay more under James I they objected strongly. These

objections have usually been assessed by historians in political and constitutional terms but they must also have reflected strong dislike of the financial implications of demands, in the early years of James's reign, for increased customs and feudal revenues and for the institution of a new and substantial annual tax, probably largely upon land, which was envisaged in the abortive Great Contract of 1610.[66] There is considerable irony in the fact that the man most responsible for these increased financial burdens, both those imposed and those intended, was Burghley's son and political heir, Robert Cecil.

In short term perspective Burghley's fiscal conservatism probably helped to preserve political stability; low taxation is always welcome to taxpayers. He also, however, stored up severe problems for the future. Elizabeth and he had great difficulty in financing the war effort against Spain after 1585. When England went to war again in the 1620s, in a much less favourable political climate, there was a desperate shortage of money. Burghley could have substantially raised taxation levels and still left the country much less heavily taxed than her European rivals. For that reason, and despite his preservation of the country's solvency, it can be argued that the Elizabethan financial story is one of missed opportunities for which Burghley must bear a very large part of the blame. Elizabeth and he left James I and Robert Cecil, with both a regular revenue and a potential parliamentary revenue which were a good deal smaller than they need have been.

---

66 Smith, *The Emergence of a Nation State*, 253 - 5.

# V. THE TUDOR STATESMAN

If the financial history of Elizabeth's reign was, at best, a highly qualified success story, it is difficult to deny that, in a short-term context, the Queen and Burghley accomplished their main aims.[67] They protected England's security, both at home and abroad and raised enough money to keep the country solvent. England was a stronger power, in relative terms, in 1603 than she had been in 1558 or, indeed, in 1585. Historians have differed widely in their judgments of the respective roles of the Queen and Burghley in this achievement. J.A. Froude, who, in the later 19th century, published a twelve volume history of England from 1529 to 1588, started his researches with a great admiration for the Queen, but concluded them with the belief that it was Burghley who was primarily responsible for the successes of the reign. Neale, on the other hand, although he recognized Burghley's great importance, never wavered from his view that it was the Queen who was the driving force behind England's achievements during her reign.[68]

Neither of these views is wholly convincing and it seems best to stress the temperamental similarities of Burghley and Elizabeth and to emphasize their co-operation during their long partnership. Their difference over issues like the succession and Mary Queen of Scots, which have naturally been highlighted by historians, should be

---

67 A.G.R. Smith, *Tudor Government*, especially 27ff.

68 J.A. Froude, *History of England from the fall of Wolsey to the defeat of the Spanish Armada*, 12 volumes (1856 - 70); J.E. Neale, *Queen Elizabeth*; *Elizabeth I and her Parliaments*, 2 vols.

seen as temporary - though very important - interludes in a fundamentally happy relationship. In the later years of the reign in particular, as two ageing conservatives, the Queen and Burghley usually found themselves in agreement on major issues. The fundamental contributions which they made to the Elizabethan age were so often made together that it is very difficult to give either one of them priority of achievement over the other.

Burghley deserves his traditional reputation as one of the great statesmen of the century - the length of his service, his reputation at home and abroad, his fine intellect, all contributed to the success story that was Elizabethan England. Of course, there were flaws in his performance, perhaps most of all in the financial field, and his conservatism grew more and more marked as he grew older. It made the contrast between him and that great radical statesman, Thomas Cromwell, ever more obvious. It should be remembered, however, that what Burghley was working to conserve and preserve was, in its essence, the Cromwellian state which had been established in the 1530s - a nation state subject to no outside authority. Cromwell played a crucial role in its creation, Burghley almost as important a role in its preservation.

# FURTHER READING

Three general works which put the Elizabethan period and Burghley's career in perspective are P. Williams, *The Tudor Regime* (Oxford, 1979), A.G.R. Smith, *The Emergence of a Nation State : the Commonwealth of England, 1529 - 1660* (1984), and J. Guy, *Tudor England* (Oxford, 1988). A.G.R. Smith, *The Government of Elizabethan England* (1967) is a brief introduction to the subject. The standard life of Burghley is Conyers Read's two volume study, *Mr Secretary Cecil and Queen Elizabeth* (1955), *Lord Burghley and Queen Elizabeth* (1960), a vast quarry, almost entirely narrative in approach. In contrast, in the second part of his *Burghley, Tudor Statesman* (1967), B.W. Beckingsale attempts an analytical treatment of some of the most important aspects of his subject's career and interests. J. Hurstfield's 'Burghley : William Cecil, 1520 - 1598', *History Today*, 6 (1956), is a brilliant sketch, while the same author's *The Queen's Wards* (1958), a work of much wider interest than its title suggests, contains many important insights into Burghley's work and character. A.G.R. Smith, *Servant of the Cecils : the Life of Sir Michael Hickes* (1977) is a study of one of Burghley's private secretaries which, *inter alia*, throws light on the workings of the patronage system. Smith has also edited *The 'Anonymous Life' of William Cecil, Lord Burghley* (Lampeter, 1990), the most important literary source for Burghley's career. Burghley's work in parliament can be explored from one perspective in J.E. Neale, *Elizabeth I and her Parliaments*, 2 vols (1953, 1957) and from another in G.R. Elton, *The Parliament of England, 1559 - 1581* (Cambridge, 1986) and M.A.R. Graves, *The Tudor Parliaments, 1485 - 1603* (1985), *Elizabethan Parliaments, 1559 - 1601* (1987). W.T. MacCaffrey's volumes, *The Shaping of the Elizabethan Regime 1558 - 1572* (1969) and *Queen Elizabeth and the Making of Policy 1572 - 1588* (Princeton, 1981) contain important analyses of Burghley's role in both the domestic and foreign politics of the time, while R.B.Wernham's books, *The Making of Elizabethan Foreign Policy, 1558 -1603* (Berkeley, California, 1980) *Before the Armada, 1485 - 1588* (1966) and *After the Armada, 1588 - 1595* (Oxford 1984) focus on foreign affairs. C. Wilson *Queen Elizabeth and the Revolt of the Netherlands* (1970) is an attack on Elizabeth's and Burghley's handling of English policy towards the revolt. A.G.R. Smith, *The Last Years of Mary Queen of Scots* (1990) includes a detailed discussion of Burghley's role in the events leading up to Mary's execution. J. Hurstfield's volume of essays, *Freedom, Corruption and Government in Elizabethan England* (1973) contains important pieces on 'Political corruption in Modern England' and on 'Church and State, 1559 - 1612 : the task of the Cecils'. F.C. Dietz, *English Public Finance 1558 - 1641* (2nd ed., 1964) is still the only general study of the financial history of the period and T.S. Willan, ed., *A Tudor Book of Rates* (Manchester, 1962) throws important light on the Elizabethan customs.